next

First published in Great Britain in 2009 by Parragon Books Ltd.
This edition published in 2010 exclusively for Next Retail Limited.

next.co.uk
nextflowers.co.uk

ISBN: 978-1-4454-1048-7

Printed and bound in China

Notes for the Reader
This book uses metric and imperial measurements. Follow the same units of measurement throughout; do not mix metric and imperial. All spoon measurements are level: teaspoons are assumed to be 5 ml, and tablespoons are assumed to be 15 ml. Unless otherwise stated, milk is assumed to be full fat, eggs and individual vegetables are medium, and pepper is freshly ground black pepper.

The times given are an approximate guide only. Preparation times differ according to the techniques used by different people and the cooking times may also vary from those given. Optional ingredients, variations, or serving suggestions have not been included in the calculations.

Recipes using raw or very lightly cooked eggs should be avoided by infants, the elderly, pregnant women, convalescents and anyone suffering from an illness. Pregnant and breastfeeding women are advised to avoid eating peanuts and peanut products. Sufferers from nut allergies should be aware that some of the ready-made ingredients used in the recipes in this book may contain nuts. Always check the packaging before use.

Contents

Introduction

Exquisite, individual, little and cute is probably what makes a cupcake so tempting, and being delicious too, who can resist such a treat? We all need a treat from time to time and a cupcake is the perfect answer.

There's a cupcake for every occasion and for any age, from special days, such as a child's birthday to Christmas, a wedding or Easter. They can be eaten as desserts, at coffee time, with afternoon tea or as a snack-time treat. They also make the perfect gift for those difficult-to-buy-for friends and are ideal for a cake sale. For children's parties, it is worth remembering that they can be popped straight into party bags.

The Cupcake's History

The invention of cupcakes has two sources and probably there is truth in both. One thought is credited to the fact that the ingredients were originally measured by bakers in standard-sized cups, instead of weights and measures, and proof of this is illustrated in some old cookery books. Another thought is credited to the cakes being baked in a tea cup and again, this is evident in old cookery books. Today, the term 'cupcake' is used for a small cake baked in a fluted paper or foil baking case, a cup or a cup-shaped mould. The cupcake is also sometimes called a fairy cake, probably because they are small, light and delicate, like a fairy. Their base is made with the basic plain cake mixture with a simple iced topping or a dusting of icing sugar.

The Ingredients

Cupcakes are simple and easy to make and you will probably find that you already have most of the ingredients needed to make them in your refrigerator and store cupboard. Self-raising white flour, butter or margarine, caster sugar and eggs are all that are needed for a basic mixture. The addition of chocolate or cocoa powder is always popular and other additional ingredients include vanilla, spices, fresh and dried fruits, and nuts. As with large cakes, a topping of butter cream or a decoration is characteristic of these miniature versions, so keep a supply of toppings in the store cupboard, such as sprinkles, hundreds and thousands, sugar strands, silver or gold dragées, chocolate flowers and edible sugar flower shapes.

The Basic Cupcake Recipe

If you want to make up a batch for your own creations, this is the basic mixture that will make 12 standard-sized cupcakes: 115 g/4 oz softened butter or soft tub margarine, 115 g/4 oz caster sugar, 115 g/4 oz self-raising white flour and 2 eggs. For a chocolate mixture, replace 1 tablespoon of the flour with 1 tablespoon cocoa powder. Fill the paper cases about two-thirds full and bake in the oven at 180°C/350°F/Gas Mark 4 for about 20 minutes. To make sufficient butter cream icing to top them, you will need 85 g/3 oz butter and 175 g/6 oz icing sugar. For a glacé icing you will need 175 g/6 oz icing sugar and 2–3 teaspoons water.

Baking Cupcakes

Cupcakes are best when freshly baked and baked in a fluted paper or foil baking case. These not only retain the cakes and make them an ideal individual serving, but also help to keep them moist and fresh for longer. They are available in mini, standard and large (muffin) sizes in a variety of colours and decorations. Reusable, silicone baking cases in bright colours are also available.

Perfect Results

Baking cupcakes is a science as well as an art, so unless you are very experienced in baking generally, it is important to follow the recipes exactly. Read through the recipe and collect all the ingredients and equipment together before you start – this will make the process of baking the cupcakes a lot easier. Do not be tempted to cut corners. It is worth noting that there may be some variables that may affect the end result and the biggest of these is usually the oven. Because temperatures can vary from appliance to appliance, to ensure the best results, use the baking times specified in the recipes as a guide only. Do not be tempted to check the oven too early, which could adversely affect the cupcakes, but do check just a few minutes before the end of the baking time to see how the cupcakes are progressing.

Equipment

Measuring scales, mixing bowls, a wooden spoon, baking trays, and bun trays are all the items you'll need to begin making cupcakes. But as soon as the baking bug bites, you can gradually add other tools to those basics, such as an electric whisk, which will certainly make the job easier and quicker.

1

Fun &
Fancy

Pink & White Cupcakes

makes 16

115 g/4 oz self-raising flour

1 tsp baking powder

115 g/4 oz butter, softened

115 g/4 oz caster sugar

2 eggs, lightly beaten

1 tbsp milk

few drops red food colouring

for the topping

1 egg white

175 g/6 oz caster sugar

2 tbsp hot water

large pinch of cream of tartar

2 tbsp raspberry jam

3 tbsp desiccated coconut, lightly toasted

Preheat the oven to 180°C/350°F/Gas Mark 4. Put 16 paper baking cases in 2 bun trays or put 16 double-layer paper cases on a large baking tray.

Sift the flour and baking powder into a bowl. Add the butter, sugar and eggs and, using an electric hand whisk, beat together until smooth. Mix together the milk and food colouring and whisk into the mixture until evenly blended. Spoon the mixture into the paper cases.

Bake the cupcakes in the preheated oven for 20 minutes or until risen and golden brown. Transfer to a wire rack and leave to cool.

To make the topping, put the egg white, sugar, water and cream of tartar in a heatproof bowl set over a saucepan of simmering water. Using an electric hand whisk, beat for 5–6 minutes until the mixture is thick and softly peaks when the whisk is lifted.

Spread a layer of raspberry jam over each cupcake then swirl over the frosting. Sprinkle with the toasted coconut.

Rose Petal Cupcakes

makes 12

115 g/4 oz butter, softened

115 g/4 oz caster sugar

2 eggs, lightly beaten

1 tbsp milk

few drops of essence of rose oil

¼ tsp vanilla extract

175 g/6 oz self-raising flour

crystallized rose petals and silver dragées (cake decoration balls), to decorate

for the icing

85 g/3 oz butter, softened

175 g/6 oz icing sugar

pink or purple food colouring (optional)

Preheat the oven to 200°C/400°F/Gas Mark 6. Put 12 paper baking cases in a bun tray, or put 12 double-layer paper cases on a baking tray.

Put the butter and sugar in a bowl and beat together until light and fluffy. Gradually add the eggs, beating well after each addition. Stir in the milk, rose essence and vanilla extract then, using a metal spoon, fold in the flour. Spoon the mixture into the paper cases and bake the cupcakes in the preheated oven for 12–15 minutes until well risen and golden brown. Transfer to a wire rack and leave to cool.

To make the icing, put the butter in a large bowl and beat until fluffy. Sift in the icing sugar and mix well together. If wished, add a few drops of pink or purple food colouring to complement the rose petals.

When the cupcakes are cold, spread the icing on top of each cake. Top with 1–2 crystallized rose petals and sprinkle with silver dragées to decorate.

Poppy Seed & Orange Cupcakes

makes 12

2 tbsp poppy seeds

2 tbsp hot milk

85 g/3 oz butter, softened

85 g/3 oz caster sugar

finely grated rind of
½ orange

1 large egg, lightly beaten

100 g/3½ oz self-raising
flour

for the icing

85 g/3 oz butter, softened

finely grated rind of
½ orange

175 g/6 oz icing sugar

1–2 tbsp orange juice

Preheat the oven to 180°C/350°F/Gas Mark 4. Put 12 paper baking cases in a bun tray or put 12 double-layer paper cases on a baking tray. Place the poppy seeds and milk in a small bowl and set aside for 10 minutes.

Put the butter, sugar and orange rind in a bowl and beat together until light and fluffy. Gradually beat in the egg. Sift in the flour and, using a metal spoon, fold gently into the mixture with the poppy seeds and milk. Spoon the mixture into the paper cases.

Bake the cupcakes in the preheated oven for 20 minutes or until risen and golden brown. Transfer to a wire rack and leave to cool.

To make the icing, put the butter and orange rind in a bowl and beat until fluffy. Gradually beat in the icing sugar and enough orange juice to make a smooth and creamy icing. Swirl the icing over the top of the cupcakes.

Fairy Cupcakes

makes 16

115 g/4 oz unsalted butter

115 g/4 oz caster sugar

2 eggs, beaten

115 g/4 oz self-raising flour

sugar flowers, hundreds and thousands, glacé cherries, and/ or chocolate strands, to decorate

for the icing

200 g/7 oz icing sugar

about 2 tbsp warm water

a few drops of food colouring (optional)

Preheat the oven to 190°C/375°F/Gas Mark 5. Put 16 paper baking cases in 2 bun trays or put 2 double-layer paper cases on a baking tray.

Place the butter and caster sugar in a large bowl and cream together with a wooden spoon or electric hand whisk until pale and fluffy.

Gradually add the eggs, beating well after each addition. Fold in the flour lightly and evenly using a metal spoon. Spoon the mixture into the paper cases and bake in the preheated oven for 15–20 minutes. Cool on a wire rack.

For the icing, sift the icing sugar into a bowl and stir in just enough water to mix to a smooth paste that is thick enough to coat the back of a wooden spoon. Stir in a few drops of food colouring, if using, then spread the icing over the fairy cakes and decorate as desired.

Caramel Cupcakes

makes 12

85 g/3 oz butter, softened

55 g/2 oz soft dark brown sugar

1 tbsp golden syrup

1 large egg, lightly beaten

100 g/3½ oz self-raising flour

1 tsp grated nutmeg

2 tbsp milk

for the frosting

115 g/4 oz soft light brown sugar

1 small egg white

1 tbsp hot water

pinch of cream of tartar

Preheat the oven to 180°C/350°F/Gas Mark 4. Put 12 paper baking cases in a bun tray or put 12 double-layer paper cases on a baking tray.

Put the butter, sugar and golden syrup in a bowl and beat together until light and fluffy. Gradually beat in the egg. Sift in the flour and, using a metal spoon, fold gently into the mixture with the nutmeg and milk. Spoon the mixture into the paper cases.

Bake the cupcakes in the preheated oven for 15–20 minutes or until risen and golden brown. Transfer to a wire rack and leave to cool.

To make the frosting, put all the ingredients in a heatproof bowl set over a saucepan of simmering water. Using an electric hand whisk beat for 5–6 minutes until the mixture is thick and softly peaking when the whisk is lifted. Swirl the frosting over the cupcakes.

Drizzled Honey Cupcakes

makes 12

85 g/3 oz self-raising flour

¼ tsp ground cinnamon

pinch of ground cloves

pinch of grated nutmeg

85 g/3 oz butter, softened

85 g/3 oz caster sugar

1 tbsp clear honey

finely grated rind of
1 orange

2 eggs, lightly beaten

40 g/1½ oz walnut pieces,
finely chopped

for the topping

15 g/½ oz walnut pieces,
finely chopped

¼ tsp ground cinnamon

2 tbsp clear honey

juice of 1 orange

Preheat the oven to 190°C/375°F/Gas Mark 5. Put 12 paper baking cases in a bun tray, or put 12 double-layer paper cases on a baking tray.

Sift the flour, cinnamon, cloves and nutmeg together into a bowl. Put the butter and sugar in a separate bowl and beat together until light and fluffy. Beat in the honey and orange rind, then gradually add the eggs, beating well after each addition. Using a metal spoon, fold in the flour mixture. Stir in the walnuts, then spoon the mixture into the paper cases.

Bake the cupcakes in the preheated oven for 20 minutes, or until well risen and golden brown. Transfer to a wire rack and leave to cool.

To make the topping, mix together the walnuts and cinnamon. Put the honey and orange juice in a saucepan and heat gently, stirring, until combined.

When the cupcakes have almost cooled, prick the tops all over with a fork or skewer and then drizzle with the warm honey mixture. Sprinkle the walnut mixture over the top of each cupcake and serve warm or cold.

Mini Sweetie Cupcakes

makes 18

55 g/2 oz self-raising flour

¼ tsp baking powder

55 g/2 oz soft tub margarine

55 g/2 oz caster sugar

1 egg, lightly beaten

sweets such as dolly mixtures and smarties, to decorate

for the icing

85 g/3 oz icing sugar

2–3 tsp water

few drops pink food colouring

Preheat the oven to 180°C/350°F/Gas Mark 4. Put 18 paper mini muffin cases on a baking tray.

Sift the flour and baking powder into a bowl. Add the margarine, sugar and egg and, using an electric hand whisk, beat together until smooth. Spoon the mixture into the paper cases.

Bake the cupcakes in the preheated oven for 15–20 minutes until risen and golden brown. Transfer to a wire rack and leave to cool.

To make the icing, sift the icing sugar into a bowl and beat in the water to make a smooth thick icing. Stir in the pink food colouring. Spoon a little icing in the centre of each cupcake and decorate each with a sweet. Leave to set.

Frosted Peanut Butter Cupcakes

makes 16

55 g/2 oz butter, softened

225 g/8 oz soft light brown sugar

115 g/4 oz crunchy peanut butter

2 eggs, lightly beaten

1 tsp vanilla extract

225 g/8 oz plain white flour

2 tsp baking powder

100 ml/3½ fl oz milk

for the frosting

200 g/7 oz full-fat soft cream cheese

25 g/1 oz butter, softened

225 g/8 oz icing sugar

Preheat the oven to 180°C/350°F/Gas Mark 4. Put 16 paper baking cases in 2 bun trays or put 16 double-layer paper cases on a baking tray.

Put the butter, sugar and peanut butter in a bowl and beat together for 1–2 minutes, or until well mixed. Gradually add the eggs, beating well after each addition, then add the vanilla extract. Sift in the flour and baking powder and then, using a metal spoon, fold them into the mixture, alternating with the milk. Spoon the mixture into the paper cases.

Bake the cupcakes in the preheated oven for 25 minutes, or until well risen and golden brown. Transfer to a wire rack and leave to cool.

To make the frosting, put the cream cheese and butter in a large bowl and, using an electric hand whisk, beat together until smooth. Sift the icing sugar into the mixture, then beat together until well mixed.

When the cupcakes are cold, spread the frosting on top of each cupcake, swirling it with a round-bladed knife. Store the cupcakes in the refrigerator until ready to serve.

Chewy Flapjack Cupcakes

makes 8

40 g/1½ oz soft tub margarine

40 g/1½ oz demerara sugar

1 tbsp golden syrup

55 g/2 oz rolled oats

55 g/2 oz butter, softened

55 g/2 oz golden caster sugar

1 large egg, lightly beaten

55 g/2 oz self-raising flour

Preheat the oven to 190°C/375°F/Gas Mark 5. Put 8 paper baking cases in a bun tray or put 8 double-layer paper cases on a baking tray.

Place the margarine, demerara sugar and golden syrup in a small saucepan and heat gently until the margarine has melted. Stir in the oats. Set aside.

Put the butter and sugar in a bowl and beat together until light and fluffy. Gradually beat in the egg. Sift in the flour and, using a metal spoon, fold gently into the mixture. Spoon the mixture into the paper cases. Gently spoon the flapjack mixture over the top.

Bake the cupcakes in the preheated oven for 20 minutes or until golden brown. Transfer to a wire rack and leave to cool.

Queen Cupcakes

makes 18

115 g/4 oz butter, softened

115 g/4 oz caster sugar

2 large eggs, lightly beaten

4 tsp lemon juice

175 g/6 oz self-raising flour

115 g/4 oz currants

2–4 tbsp milk, if necessary

Preheat the oven to 190°C/375°F/Gas Mark 5. Put 18 paper baking cases in 2 bun trays, or 18 double-layer paper cases on a baking tray.

Put the butter and sugar in a bowl and beat together until light and fluffy. Gradually beat in the eggs, then beat in the lemon juice with 1 tablespoon of the flour. Using a metal spoon, fold in the remaining flour and the currants, adding a little milk, if necessary, to give a soft dropping consistency. Spoon the mixture into the paper cases.

Bake the cupcakes in the preheated oven for 15–20 minutes, or until well risen and golden brown. Transfer to a wire rack and leave to cool.

Fudge & Raisin Cupcakes

makes 10

115 g/4 oz vanilla fudge, cut into small chunks

1 tbsp milk

85 g/3 oz butter, softened

40 g/1½ oz soft light brown sugar

1 large egg, lightly beaten

100 g/3½ oz self-raising flour

25 g/1 oz raisins

Preheat the oven to 190°C/375°F/Gas Mark 5. Put 10 paper baking cases in a bun tray or put 10 double-layer paper cases on a baking tray.

Put half the fudge in a heatproof bowl with the milk and set over a saucepan of gently simmering water and leave until the fudge has melted. Remove from the heat and stir until smooth. Cool for 10 minutes.

Put the butter and sugar into a bowl and beat together until light and fluffy. Gradually beat in the egg. Sift in the flour and, using a metal spoon, fold gently into the mixture with the raisins. Fold in the melted fudge. Spoon the mixture into the paper cases. Scatter the remaining fudge chunks over the cupcakes.

Bake the cupcakes in the preheated oven for 15–20 minutes or until risen and golden brown. Transfer to a wire rack and leave to cool.

Sticky Gingerbread Cupcakes

makes 16

115 g/4 oz plain flour

2 tsp ground ginger

¾ tsp ground cinnamon

1 piece of stem ginger,
finely chopped

¾ tsp bicarbonate of soda

4 tbsp milk

85 g/3 oz butter, softened

70 g/2½ oz soft dark brown
sugar

2 tbsp black treacle

2 eggs, lightly beaten

1 piece of stem ginger,
to decorate

for the icing

85 g/3 oz butter, softened

175 g/6 oz icing sugar

2 tbsp ginger syrup from
the stem ginger jar

Preheat the oven to 160°C/325°F/Gas Mark 3. Put 16 paper baking cases in 2 bun trays, or place 16 double-layer paper cases on a baking tray.

Sift the flour, ground ginger and cinnamon together into a bowl. Add the chopped ginger and toss in the flour mixture until well coated. In a separate bowl, dissolve the bicarbonate of soda in the milk.

Put the butter and sugar in a bowl and beat together until fluffy. Beat in the treacle, then gradually add the eggs, beating well after each addition. Beat in the flour mixture, then gradually beat in the milk. Spoon the mixture into the paper cases.

Bake the cupcakes in the preheated oven for 20 minutes, or until well risen and golden brown. Transfer to a wire rack and leave to cool.

To make the icing, put the butter in a bowl and beat until fluffy. Sift in the icing sugar, add the ginger syrup and beat together until smooth and creamy. Slice the stem ginger into thin slivers or chop finely.

When the cupcakes are cold, spread the icing on top of each cupcake, then decorate with pieces of the ginger.

Iced Madeira Cupcakes

makes 16

115 g/4 oz butter, softened

115 g/4 oz golden caster sugar

finely grated rind of ½ lemon

2 large eggs, lightly beaten

175 g/6 oz self-raising flour

40 g/1½ oz ground almonds

55 g/2 oz candied citron peel, thinly sliced

for the icing

55 g/2 oz icing sugar

3 tsp warm water

Preheat the oven to 180°C/350°F/Gas Mark 4. Put 16 paper baking cases in 2 bun trays or put 16 double-layer paper cases on a baking tray.

Put the butter, sugar and lemon rind in a bowl and beat together until light and fluffy. Gradually beat in the eggs. Sift in the flour and, using a metal spoon, fold gently into the mixture with the ground almonds. Spoon the mixture into the paper cases. Put a slice of citron peel on the top of each cupcake.

Bake the cupcakes in the preheated oven for 20–25 minutes or until risen and golden brown. Transfer to a wire rack and leave to cool.

To make the icing, sift the icing sugar into a bowl and add enough of the warm water to make a runny icing. Using a pastry brush, glaze the top of each cupcake with the icing. Leave to set.

Rocky Road Cupcakes

makes 12

2 tbsp cocoa powder

2 tbsp hot water

115 g/4 oz butter, softened

115 g/4 oz caster sugar

2 eggs, lightly beaten

115 g/4 oz self-raising flour

for the topping

25 g/1 oz chopped mixed nuts

100 g/3½ oz milk chocolate, melted

115 g/4 oz mini marshmallows

40 g/1½ oz glacé cherries, chopped

Preheat the oven to 180°C/350°F/Gas Mark 4. Put 12 paper muffin cases in a muffin tray.

Blend the cocoa powder and hot water together and set aside. Put the butter and sugar in a bowl and beat together until light and fluffy. Gradually beat in the eggs then beat in the blended cocoa. Sift in the flour and, using a metal spoon, fold gently into the mixture. Spoon the mixture into the paper cases.

Bake the cupcakes in the preheated oven for 20 minutes or until risen and firm to the touch. Transfer to a wire rack and leave to cool.

To make the topping, stir the nuts into the melted chocolate and spread a little of the mixture over the top of the cakes. Lightly stir the marshmallows and cherries into the remaining chocolate mixture and pile on top of the cupcakes. Leave to set.

Chocolate
Heaven

Tiny Chocolate Cupcakes with Ganache Icing

makes 20

55 g/2 oz butter, softened

55 g/2 oz caster sugar

1 large egg, lightly beaten

55 g/2 oz self-raising flour

2 tbsp cocoa powder

1 tbsp milk

20 chocolate-coated coffee beans, to decorate (optional)

for the icing

100 g/3½ oz plain chocolate

100 ml/3½ fl oz double cream

Preheat the oven to 190°C/375°F/Gas Mark 5. Put 20 double-layer mini paper cases on 2 baking trays.

Put the butter and sugar in a bowl and beat together until light and fluffy. Gradually beat in the egg. Sift in the flour and cocoa powder and then, using a metal spoon, fold them into the mixture. Stir in the milk.

Fill a piping bag, fitted with a large plain nozzle, with the mixture and pipe it into the paper cases, filling each one until half full.

Bake the cakes in the preheated oven for 10–15 minutes, or until well risen and firm to the touch. Transfer to a wire rack to cool.

To make the icing, break the chocolate into a saucepan and add the cream. Heat gently, stirring all the time, until the chocolate has melted. Pour into a large heatproof bowl and, using an electric hand whisk, beat the mixture for 10 minutes, or until thick, glossy and cool.

Fill a piping bag, fitted with a large star nozzle, with the icing and pipe a swirl on top of each cupcake. Alternatively, spoon the icing over the top of each cupcake. Chill in the refrigerator for 1 hour before serving. Serve decorated with a chocolate-coated coffee bean, if desired.

Double Chocolate Cupcakes

makes 18

85 g/3 oz white chocolate

1 tbsp milk

115 g/4 oz self-raising flour

½ tsp baking powder

115 g/4 oz butter, softened

115 g/4 oz caster sugar

2 eggs

1 tsp vanilla extract

for the topping

140 g/5 oz milk chocolate

18 white chocolate buttons

Preheat the oven to 190°C/375°F/Gas Mark 5. Put 18 paper baking cases in 2 bun trays, or put 18 double-layer paper cases on a large baking tray.

Break the white chocolate into a heatproof bowl and add the milk. Set the bowl over a saucepan of simmering water and heat until melted. Remove from the heat and stir gently until smooth.

Sift the flour and baking powder into a bowl. Add the butter, sugar, eggs and vanilla extract and, using an electric hand whisk, beat together until smooth. Fold in the melted white chocolate. Spoon the mixture into the paper cases.

Bake in the preheated oven for 20 minutes or until risen and golden brown. Transfer to a wire rack and leave to cool.

To make the topping, break the chocolate into a heatproof bowl and set the bowl over a saucepan of gently simmering water until melted. Cool for 5 minutes then spread over the top of the cupcakes. Decorate each cupcake with a chocolate button.

Mocha Cupcakes with Whipped Cream

makes 20

2 tbsp instant espresso coffee powder

85 g/3 oz butter, softened

85 g/3 oz caster sugar

1 tbsp clear honey

200 ml/7 fl oz water

225 g/8 oz plain flour

2 tbsp cocoa powder

1 tsp bicarbonate of soda

3 tbsp milk

1 large egg, lightly beaten

for the topping

225 ml/8 fl oz whipping cream

cocoa powder, sifted, for dusting

Preheat the oven to 180°C/350°F/Gas Mark 4. Put 20 paper baking cases in 2 bun trays, or put 20 double-layer paper cases on 2 baking trays.

Put the coffee powder, butter, sugar, honey and water in a saucepan and heat gently, stirring, until the sugar has dissolved. Bring to the boil, then reduce the heat and simmer for 5 minutes. Pour into a large heatproof bowl and leave to cool.

When the mixture has cooled, sift in the flour and cocoa powder. Dissolve the bicarbonate of soda in the milk, then add to the mixture with the egg and beat together until smooth. Spoon the mixture into the paper cases.

Bake the cupcakes in the preheated oven for 15–20 minutes, or until well risen and firm to the touch. Transfer to a wire rack to cool.

For the topping, whisk the cream in a bowl until it holds its shape. Just before serving, spoon heaped teaspoonfuls of cream on top of each cake, then dust lightly with sifted cocoa powder. You can store the cupcakes, without the topping, in the refrigerator until ready to serve.

Chocolate Hazelnut Cupcakes

makes 18

175 g/6 oz butter, softened

115 g/4 oz light soft brown sugar

2 large eggs, lightly beaten

2 tbsp chocolate and hazelnut spread

175 g/6 oz self-raising flour

50 g/2 oz blanched hazelnuts, roughly ground

for the topping

5 tbsp chocolate and hazelnut spread

18 whole blanched hazelnuts

Preheat the oven to 180°C/350°F/Gas Mark 4. Put 18 paper baking cases in 2 bun trays or put 18 double-layer paper cases on a large baking tray.

Put the butter and sugar in a mixing bowl and beat together until light and fluffy. Gradually beat in the eggs then stir in the chocolate and hazelnut spread. Sift in the flour and, using a metal spoon, fold into the mixture with the ground hazelnuts. Spoon the mixture into the paper cases.

Bake the cupcakes in the preheated oven for 20–25 minutes or until risen and firm to the touch. Transfer to a wire rack and leave to cool.

When the cupcakes are cold, swirl some chocolate and hazelnut spread over the top of each cupcake and top with a hazelnut.

Devil's Food Cupcakes with Chocolate Icing

makes 18

50 g/1¾ oz soft tub margarine

115 g/4 oz soft dark brown sugar

2 large eggs

115 g/4 oz plain flour

½ tsp bicarbonate of soda

25 g/1 oz cocoa powder

125 ml/4 fl oz soured cream

for the icing

125 g/4½ oz plain chocolate

2 tbsp caster sugar

150 ml/5 fl oz soured cream

chocolate caraque, to decorate

Preheat the oven to 180°C/350°F/Gas Mark 4. Put 18 paper baking cases in 2 bun trays, or put 18 double-layer paper cases on a baking tray.

Put the margarine, sugar, eggs, flour, bicarbonate of soda and cocoa powder in a large bowl and, using an electric hand whisk, beat together until just smooth. Using a metal spoon, fold in the soured cream. Spoon the mixture into the paper cases.

Bake the cupcakes in the preheated oven for 20 minutes, or until well risen and firm to the touch. Transfer to a wire rack to cool.

To make the icing, break the chocolate into a heatproof bowl. Set the bowl over a saucepan of gently simmering water and heat until melted, stirring occasionally. Remove from the heat and allow to cool slightly, then whisk in the sugar and soured cream until combined. Spread the icing over the tops of the cupcakes and leave to set in the refrigerator before serving. Serve decorated with chocolate caraque.

Dark & White Fudge Cupcakes

makes 20

200 ml/7 fl oz water
85 g/3 oz butter, softened
85 g/3 oz caster sugar
1 tbsp golden syrup
3 tbsp milk
1 tsp vanilla extract
1 tsp bicarbonate of soda
225 g/8 oz plain flour
2 tbsp cocoa powder

for the topping

50 g/1¾ oz plain chocolate
4 tbsp water
50 g/1¾ oz butter
50 g/1¾ oz white chocolate
350 g/12 oz icing sugar

for the chocolate curls

100 g/3½ oz plain chocolate
100 g/3½ oz white chocolate

Preheat the oven to 180°C/350°F/Gas Mark 4. Put 20 paper baking cases in 2 bun trays, or put 20 double-layer paper cases on 2 baking trays.

Put the water, butter, sugar and syrup in a saucepan. Heat gently, stirring, until the sugar has dissolved, then bring to the boil. Reduce the heat and cook gently for 5 minutes. Remove from the heat and leave to cool.

Meanwhile, put the milk and vanilla extract in a bowl. Add the bicarbonate of soda and stir to dissolve. Sift the flour and cocoa powder into a separate bowl and add the syrup mixture. Stir in the milk and beat until smooth. Spoon the mixture into the paper cases until they are two-thirds full.

Bake the cupcakes in the preheated oven for 20 minutes, or until well risen and firm to the touch. Transfer to a wire rack and leave to cool.

To make the topping, break the plain chocolate into a small heatproof bowl, add half the water and half the butter, and set the bowl over a saucepan of gently simmering water until melted. Stir until smooth and leave to stand over the water. Repeat with the white chocolate and remaining water and butter. Sift half the icing sugar into each bowl and beat until smooth and thick. Top the cupcakes up with the icings. Leave to set. Serve decorated with chocolate curls made by shaving the chocolate with a potato peeler.

Chocolate & Orange Cupcakes

makes 16

115 g/4 oz butter, softened

115 g/4 oz golden caster sugar

finely grated rind and juice ½ orange

2 eggs, lightly beaten

115 g/4 oz self-raising flour

25 g/1 oz plain chocolate, grated

for the icing

115 g/4 oz plain chocolate, broken into pieces

25 g/1 oz unsalted butter

1 tbsp golden syrup

thin strips candied orange peel, to decorate

Preheat the oven to 180°C/350°F/Gas Mark 4. Put 16 paper baking cases in 2 bun trays or put 16 double-layer paper cases on a baking tray.

Put the butter, sugar and orange rind in a bowl and beat together until light and fluffy. Gradually beat in the eggs. Sift in the flour and, using a metal spoon, fold gently into the mixture with the orange juice and grated chocolate. Spoon the mixture into the paper cases.

Bake the cupcakes in the preheated oven for 20 minutes or until risen and golden brown. Transfer to a wire rack and leave to cool.

To make the icing, break the chocolate into a heatproof bowl and add the butter and syrup. Set the bowl over a saucepan of simmering water and heat until melted. Remove from the heat and stir until smooth. Cool until the icing is thick enough to spread. Spread over the cupcakes and decorate each cupcake with a few strips of candied orange peel. Leave to set.

Marbled Chocolate Cupcakes

makes 21

175 g/6 oz soft tub margarine

175 g/6 oz caster sugar

3 eggs

175 g/6 oz self-raising flour

2 tbsp milk

55 g/2 oz plain chocolate, melted

Preheat the oven to 180°C/350°F/Gas Mark 4. Put 21 paper baking cases in 2 bun trays, or put 21 double-layer paper cases on 2 baking trays.

Put the margarine, sugar, eggs, flour and milk in a large bowl and, using an electric hand whisk, beat together until just smooth.

Divide the mixture between 2 bowls. Add the melted chocolate to one bowl and stir until well mixed. Using a teaspoon, and alternating the chocolate mixture with the plain mixture, put four half-teaspoons into each paper case.

Bake the cupcakes in the preheated oven for 20 minutes, or until well risen and springy to the touch. Transfer to a wire rack and leave to cool.

Pear & Chocolate Cupcakes

makes 12

115 g/4 oz soft tub margarine

115 g/4 oz light soft brown sugar

2 eggs

100 g/3½ oz self-raising flour

½ tsp baking powder

2 tbsp cocoa powder

4 canned pear halves, drained and sliced

2 tbsp runny honey, warmed

Preheat the oven to 190°C/375°F/Gas Mark 5. Put 12 paper baking cases in a bun tray or put 12 double-layer paper cases on a baking tray.

Put the margarine, sugar, eggs, flour, baking powder and cocoa powder in a large bowl and, using an electric hand whisk, beat together until just smooth. Spoon the mixture into the paper cases and smooth the tops. Arrange 2 pear slices on top of each cupcake.

Bake the cupcakes in the preheated oven for 20 minutes or until risen and just firm to the touch. Transfer to a wire cooling rack. Whilst the cupcakes are still warm, glaze with the honey. Leave to cool completely.

Chocolate Butterfly Cupcakes

makes 12

125 g/4½ oz soft tub margarine

125 g/4½ oz caster sugar

150 g/5½ oz self-raising flour

2 large eggs

2 tbsp cocoa powder

25 g/1 oz plain chocolate, melted

icing sugar, sifted, for dusting

for the filling

85 g/3 oz butter, softened

175 g/6 oz icing sugar

25 g/1 oz plain chocolate, melted

Preheat the oven to 180°C/350°F/Gas Mark 4. Put 12 paper baking cases in a bun tray, or put 12 double-layer paper cases on a baking tray.

Put the margarine, sugar, flour, eggs and cocoa powder in a large bowl and, using an electric hand whisk, beat together until just smooth. Beat in the melted chocolate. Spoon the mixture into the paper cases, filling them three-quarters full.

Bake the cupcakes in the preheated oven for 15 minutes, or until springy to the touch. Transfer to a wire rack and leave to cool.

To make the filling, put the butter in a bowl and beat until fluffy. Sift in the icing sugar and beat together until smooth. Add the melted chocolate and beat together until well mixed.

When the cupcakes are cold, use a serrated knife to cut a circle from the top of each cake and then cut each circle in half. Spread or pipe a little of the butter cream into the centre of each cupcake and press 2 semi-circular halves into it at an angle to resemble butterfly wings. Dust with sifted icing sugar before serving.

Chocolate Cupcakes with Cream Cheese Icing

makes 18

85 g/3 oz butter, softened

100 g/3½ oz caster sugar

2 eggs, lightly beaten

2 tbsp milk

55 g/2 oz plain chocolate chips

225 g/8 oz self-raising flour

25 g/1 oz cocoa powder

for the icing

225 g/8 oz white chocolate

150 g/5½ oz low-fat cream cheese

chocolate curls, to decorate

Preheat the oven to 200°C/400°F/Gas Mark 6. Put 18 paper baking cases in 2 bun trays, or put 18 double-layer paper cases on a baking tray.

Put the butter and sugar in a bowl and beat together until light and fluffy. Gradually add the eggs, beating well after each addition. Add the milk, then fold in the chocolate chips. Sift the flour and cocoa powder together, then fold into the mixture. Spoon the mixture into the paper cases and smooth the tops.

Bake the cupcakes in the preheated oven for 20 minutes, or until well risen and springy to the touch. Transfer to a wire rack and leave to cool.

To make the icing, break the chocolate into a small heatproof bowl and set the bowl over a saucepan of gently simmering water until melted. Leave to cool slightly. Put the cream cheese in a bowl and beat until softened, then beat in the slightly cooled chocolate.

Spread a little of the icing over the top of each cupcake, then leave to chill in the refrigerator for 1 hour before serving. Serve decorated with the chocolate curls.

Chocolate Chip Cupcakes

makes 8

100 g/3½ oz soft tub margarine

100 g/3½ oz caster sugar

2 large eggs

100 g/3½ oz self-raising flour

100 g/3½ oz plain chocolate chips

Preheat the oven to 190°C/375°F/Gas Mark 5. Put 8 paper baking cases in a bun tray or put 8 double-layer paper cases on a baking tray.

Put the margarine, sugar, eggs and flour in a large bowl and, using an electric hand whisk, beat together until just smooth. Fold in the chocolate chips. Spoon the mixture into the paper cases.

Bake the cupcakes in the preheated oven for 20–25 minutes, or until well risen and golden brown. Transfer to a wire rack to cool.

Chocolate Florentine Cupcakes

makes 12

55 g/2 oz plain chocolate

85 g/3 oz butter, softened

1 tbsp golden syrup

55 g/2 oz light soft brown sugar

115 g/4 oz self-raising flour

1 large egg, beaten

for the topping

40 g/1½ oz glace cherries, chopped

25 g/1 oz flaked almonds

1 tbsp raisins

1 tbsp golden syrup

Preheat the oven to 190°C/375°F/Gas Mark 5. Put 12 paper baking cases in a bun tray or put 12 double-layer paper cases on a baking tray.

Put the chocolate, butter, golden syrup and sugar in a saucepan and heat gently, stirring occasionally, until just melted. Cool for 2 minutes. Sift the flour into a bowl.

Pour the chocolate mixture into the bowl. Add the egg and beat until thoroughly blended. Spoon the mixture into the paper cases.

Mix together the topping ingredients and gently spoon a little of the mixture on top of each cupcake.

Bake the cupcakes in the preheated oven for 15–20 minutes or until risen and firm to the touch. Transfer to a wire rack and leave to cool.

Fruit & Nut

Lemon Butterfly Cupcakes

makes 12

115 g/4 oz self-raising flour

½ tsp baking powder

115 g/4 oz soft tub margarine

115 g/4 oz caster sugar

2 eggs, lightly beaten

finely grated rind of ½ lemon

2 tbsp milk

icing sugar, for dusting

for the lemon filling

85 g/3 oz butter, softened

175/6 oz icing sugar

1 tbsp lemon juice

Preheat the oven to 190°C/375°F/Gas Mark 5. Put 12 paper baking cases in a bun tray, or put 12 double-layer paper cases on a baking tray.

Sift the flour and baking powder into a large bowl. Add the margarine, sugar, eggs, lemon rind and milk and, using an electric hand whisk, beat together until smooth. Spoon the mixture into the paper cases.

Bake the cupcakes in the preheated oven for 15–20 minutes, or until well risen and golden brown. Transfer to a wire rack and leave to cool.

To make the filling, put the butter in a bowl and beat until fluffy. Sift in the icing sugar, add the lemon juice and beat together until smooth and creamy.

When the cupcakes are cold, use a serrated knife to cut a circle from the top of each cupcake and then cut each circle in half. Spread or pipe a little of the butter-cream filling into the centre of each cupcake, then press 2 semi-circular halves into it at an angle to resemble butterfly wings. Dust with sifted icing sugar before serving.

Tropical Pineapple Cupcakes with Citrus Cream Frosting

makes 12

2 slices of canned pineapple in natural juice

85 g/3 oz butter, softened

85 g/3 oz caster sugar

1 large egg, lightly beaten

85 g/3 oz self-raising flour

1 tbsp juice from the canned pineapple

for the frosting

25 g/1 oz butter, softened

100 g/3½ oz soft cream cheese

grated rind of 1 lemon or lime

100 g/3½ oz icing sugar

1 tsp lemon juice or lime juice

Preheat the oven to 180°C/350°F/Gas Mark 4. Put 12 paper baking cases in a bun tray, or put 12 double-layer paper cases on a baking tray.

Finely chop the pineapple slices. Put the butter and sugar in a bowl and beat together until light and fluffy. Gradually beat in the egg. Add the flour and, using a large metal spoon, fold into the mixture. Fold in the chopped pineapple and the pineapple juice. Spoon the mixture into the paper cases.

Bake the cupcakes in the preheated oven for 20 minutes, or until well risen and golden brown. Transfer to a wire rack and leave to cool.

To make the frosting, put the butter and cream cheese in a large bowl and, using an electric hand whisk, beat together until smooth. Add the rind from the lemon or lime. Sift the icing sugar into the mixture, then beat together until well mixed. Gradually beat in the juice from the lemon or lime, adding enough to form a spreading consistency.

When the cupcakes are cold, spread the frosting on top of each cake, or fill a piping bag fitted with a large star nozzle and pipe the frosting on top. Store the cupcakes in the refrigerator until ready to serve.

Macadamia & Maple Cupcakes

makes 10

85 g/3 oz butter, softened

55 g/2 oz light soft brown sugar

2 tbsp maple syrup

1 large egg, lightly beaten

85 g/3 oz self-raising flour

55 g/2 oz macadamia nuts, chopped

1 tbsp milk

for the frosting

25 g/1 oz butter, softened

2 tbsp maple syrup

85 g/3 oz icing sugar, sifted

85 g/3 oz cream cheese

2 tbsp chopped macadamia nuts, lightly toasted

Preheat the oven to 190°C/375°F/Gas Mark 5. Put 10 paper baking cases in a bun tray or put 10 double-layer paper cases on a baking tray.

Put the butter, sugar and maple syrup in a bowl and beat together until light and fluffy. Gradually beat in the egg. Sift in the flour and, using a metal spoon, fold into the mixture with the nuts and milk. Spoon the mixture into the paper cases.

Bake the cupcakes in the preheated oven for 20 minutes or until golden brown and firm to the touch. Transfer to a wire rack and leave to cool.

To make the frosting, beat the butter and maple syrup together until smooth. Sift in the icing sugar and beat in thoroughly. Gently beat in the cream cheese. Swirl the icing on the top of each cake and sprinkle over the toasted nuts.

Cranberry Cupcakes

makes 14

75 g/2¾ oz butter, softened

100 g/3½ oz caster sugar

1 large egg

2 tbsp milk

100 g/3½ oz self-raising flour

1 tsp baking powder

75 g/2¾ oz cranberries, frozen

Preheat the oven to 180°C/350°F/Gas Mark 4. Put 14 paper baking cases in 2 bun trays, or put 14 double-layer paper cases on a baking tray.

Put the butter and sugar in a bowl and beat together until light and fluffy. Gradually beat in the egg, then stir in the milk. Sift in the flour and baking powder and, using a large metal spoon, fold them into the mixture. Gently fold in the frozen cranberries. Spoon the mixture into the paper cases.

Bake the cupcakes in the preheated oven for 15–20 minutes, or until well risen and golden brown. Transfer to a wire rack and leave to cool.

Apple Streusel Cupcakes

makes 14

½ tsp bicarbonate of soda

280 g/10 oz jar Bramley apple sauce

55 g/2 oz butter, softened

85 g/3 oz demerara sugar

1 large egg, lightly beaten

175 g/6 oz self-raising flour

½ tsp ground cinnamon

½ tsp freshly ground nutmeg

for the topping

50 g/1¾ oz plain white flour

50 g/1¾ oz demerara sugar

¼ tsp ground cinnamon

¼ tsp freshly grated nutmeg

35 g/1¼ oz butter

Preheat the oven to 180°C/350°F/Gas Mark 4. Put 14 paper baking cases in 2 bun trays, or put 14 double-layer paper cases on a baking tray.

First make the topping. Put the flour, sugar, cinnamon and nutmeg in a bowl or in the bowl of a food processor. Cut the butter into small pieces, then either rub it in by hand or blend in the processor until the mixture resembles fine breadcrumbs. Set aside while you make the cakes.

To make the cupcakes, add the bicarbonate of soda to the jar of Bramley apple sauce and stir until dissolved. Put the butter and sugar in a bowl and beat together until light and fluffy. Gradually beat in the egg. Sift in the flour, cinnamon and nutmeg and, using a large metal spoon, fold into the mixture, alternating with the apple sauce.

Spoon the mixture into the paper cases. Scatter the topping over each cupcake to cover the tops and press down gently.

Bake the cupcakes in the preheated oven for 20 minutes, or until well risen and golden brown. Leave the cakes for 2–3 minutes before serving warm or transfer to a wire rack and leave to cool.

Carrot & Orange Cupcakes with Mascarpone Icing

makes 12

115 g/4 oz butter, softened

115 g/4 oz soft light brown sugar

juice and finely grated rind of 1 small orange

2 large eggs, lightly beaten

175 g/6 oz carrots, grated

25 g/1 oz walnut pieces, roughly chopped

125 g/4½ oz plain flour

1 tsp ground mixed spice

1½ tsp baking powder

for the icing

280 g/10 oz mascarpone cheese

4 tbsp icing sugar

grated rind of 1 large orange

Preheat the oven to 180°C/350°F/Gas Mark 4. Put 12 paper baking cases in a bun tray or put 12 double-layer paper cases on a baking tray.

Put the butter, sugar and orange rind in a bowl and beat together until light and fluffy. Gradually add the eggs, beating well after each addition. Squeeze any excess liquid from the carrots and add to the mixture with the walnuts and orange juice. Stir into the mixture until well mixed. Sift the flour, mixed spice and baking powder and then, using a metal spoon, fold into the mixture. Spoon the mixture into the paper cases.

Bake the cupcakes in the preheated oven for 25 minutes, or until well risen, firm to the touch and golden brown. Transfer to a wire rack and leave to cool. To make the icing, put the mascarpone cheese, icing sugar and orange rind in a large bowl and beat together until well mixed.

When the cupcakes are cold, spread the icing on top of each cupcake, swirling it with a round-bladed knife. Store the cupcakes in the refrigerator until ready to serve.

Mango & Passion Fruit Cupcakes

makes 18

115 g/4 oz butter, softened

115 g/4 oz caster sugar

1 tsp finely grated orange rind

2 eggs, lightly beaten

115 g/4 oz self-raising flour

55 g/2 oz dried mango, finely chopped

1 tbsp orange juice

for the icing

200 g/7 oz icing sugar

seeds and pulp from 1 passion fruit

2 tbsp orange juice

Preheat the oven to 190°C/375°F/Gas Mark 5. Put 18 paper baking cases in 2 bun trays or put 18 double-layer paper cases on a baking tray.

Put the butter, sugar and orange rind in a mixing bowl and beat together until light and fluffy. Gradually beat in the eggs. Sift in the flour and, using a metal spoon, fold into the mixture with the chopped mango and orange juice. Spoon the mixture into the paper cases.

Bake the cupcakes in the preheated oven for 20 minutes or until golden brown and firm to the touch. Transfer to a wire rack and leave to cool.

To make the icing, sift the icing sugar into a bowl and add the passion fruit seeds and pulp and 1 tbsp of the orange juice. Mix to a smooth icing, adding the rest of the juice if necessary. Spoon the icing over the cupcakes. Leave to set.

Shredded Orange Cupcakes

makes 12

85 g/3 oz butter, softened

85 g/3 oz caster sugar

1 large egg, lightly beaten

85 g/3 oz self-raising flour

25 g/1 oz ground almonds

grated rind and juice of
1 small orange

for the orange topping

grated rind and juice of
1 small orange

55 g/2 oz caster sugar

15 g/½ oz toasted flaked
almonds

Preheat the oven to 180°C/350°F/Gas Mark 4. Put 12 paper baking cases in a bun tray, or put 12 double-layer paper cases on a baking tray.

Put the butter and sugar in a bowl and beat together until light and fluffy. Gradually beat in the egg. Add the flour, ground almonds and orange rind and, using a large metal spoon, fold into the mixture. Fold in the orange juice. Spoon the mixture into the paper cases.

Bake the cupcakes in the preheated oven for 20–25 minutes, or until well risen and golden brown.

Meanwhile, make the topping. Put the orange rind, orange juice and sugar in a saucepan and heat gently, stirring, until the sugar has dissolved, then simmer for 5 minutes.

When the cupcakes have cooked, prick them all over with a skewer. Spoon the warm syrup and rind over each cupcake, then scatter the flaked almonds on top. Transfer to a wire rack and leave to cool.

Toffee Apple Cupcakes

makes 16

2 apples

1 tbsp lemon juice

250 g/9 oz plain flour

2 tsp baking powder

1½ tsp ground cinnamon

70 g/2½ oz light muscovado sugar

55 g/2 oz butter, plus extra for greasing

100 ml/3½ fl oz milk

100 ml/3½ fl oz apple juice

1 egg, beaten

for the toffee topping

2 tbsp single cream

40 g/1½ oz light muscovado sugar

15 g/½ oz unsalted butter

Preheat the oven to 200°C/400°F/Gas Mark 6. Put 16 paper baking cases in 2 bun trays or put 16 double-layer paper cases on a baking tray.

Core and roughly grate one of the apples. Slice the remaining apple into 5 mm/¼ inch thick wedges and toss in the lemon juice. Sift together the flour, baking powder and cinnamon, then stir in the sugar and grated apple.

Melt the butter and mix with the milk, apple juice and egg. Stir the liquid mixture into the dry ingredients, mixing lightly until just combined. Spoon the mixture into the paper cases and arrange two apple slices on top of each.

Bake in the preheated oven for 15–20 minutes or until risen, firm and golden brown. Transfer to a wire rack and leave to cool.

For the toffee topping, place all the ingredients in a small pan and heat, stirring, until the sugar is dissolved. Increase the heat and boil rapidly for 2 minutes, or until slightly thickened and syrupy. Cool slightly, then drizzle over the cakes and leave to set.

Raspberry Almond Cupcakes

makes 14

115 g/4 oz butter, softened

85 g/3 oz caster sugar

½ tsp almond extract

2 eggs, lightly beaten

85 g/3 oz self-raising flour

55 g/2 oz ground almonds

85 g/3 oz fresh raspberries

2 tbsp flaked almonds

icing sugar, to dust

Preheat the oven to 180°C/350°F/Gas Mark 4. Put 14 paper baking cases in 2 bun trays or put 14 double-layer paper cases on a baking tray.

Put the butter, sugar and almond extract in a bowl and beat together until light and fluffy. Gradually beat in the eggs. Sift in the flour and, using a metal spoon, fold into the mixture with the ground almonds. Gently fold in the raspberries. Spoon the mixture into the paper cases. Scatter the flaked almonds over the top.

Bake the cupcakes in the preheated oven for 25–30 minutes or until golden brown and firm to the touch. Transfer to a wire rack and leave to cool. Dust with icing sugar.

Black Forest Cupcakes

makes 12

85 g/3 oz plain chocolate

1 tsp lemon juice

4 tbsp milk

150 g/5½ oz self-raising flour

1 tbsp cocoa powder

½ tsp bicarbonate of soda

2 eggs

55 g/2 oz butter, softened

115 g/4 oz soft light brown sugar

25 g/1 oz dried and sweetened sour cherries, chopped

2 tbsp cherry liqueur (optional)

150 ml/5 fl oz double cream, softly whipped

5 tbsp cherry conserve

cocoa powder, to dust

Preheat the oven to 180°C/350°F/Gas Mark 4. Put 12 paper muffin cases in a muffin tray.

Break the chocolate into a heatproof bowl and set the bowl over a saucepan of gently simmering water until melted. Add the lemon juice to the milk and leave for 10 minutes – the milk will curdle a little.

Sift the flour, cocoa powder and bicarbonate of soda into a bowl. Add the eggs, butter, sugar and milk mixture and beat with an electric hand whisk until smooth. Fold in the melted chocolate and cherries. Spoon the mixture into the paper cake cases.

Bake the cupcakes in the preheated oven for 20–25 minutes until risen and firm to the touch. Transfer to a wire rack and leave to cool.

When the cupcakes are cold, use a serrated knife to cut a circle from the top of each cupcake. Sprinkle the cakes with a little cherry liqueur, if using. Spoon the whipped cream into the centres and top with a small spoonful of conserve. Gently replace the cupcake tops and dust lightly with cocoa powder. Store in the refrigerator until ready to serve.

Birthday Party Cupcakes

makes 24

225 g/8 oz soft tub margarine

225 g/8 oz caster sugar

4 eggs

225 g/8 oz self-raising flour

for the topping

175 g/6 oz butter, softened

350 g/12 oz icing sugar

a variety of small sweets and chocolates, sugar-coated chocolates, dried fruits, edible sugar flower shapes, cake decorating sprinkles, sugar strands, and hundreds and thousands

various coloured tubes of writing icing

candles and candleholders (optional)

Preheat the oven to 180°C/350°F/Gas Mark 4. Put 24 paper baking cases in 2 bun trays, or put 24 double-layer paper cases on 2 baking trays.

Put the margarine, sugar, eggs and flour in a large bowl and, using an electric hand whisk, beat together until just smooth. Spoon the mixture into the paper cases.

Bake the cupcakes in the preheated oven for 15–20 minutes, or until well risen, golden brown and firm to the touch. Transfer to a wire rack and leave to cool.

To make the icing, put the butter in a bowl and beat until fluffy. Sift in the icing sugar and beat together until smooth and creamy.

When the cupcakes are cold, spread the icing on top of each cupcake, then decorate to your choice and, if desired, place a candle in the top of each.

Halloween Cupcakes

makes 12

115 g/4 oz soft tub margarine

115 g/4 oz caster sugar

2 eggs

115 g/4 oz self-raising flour

for the topping

200 g/7 oz orange ready-to-roll coloured fondant icing

icing sugar, for dusting

55 g/2 oz black ready-to-roll coloured fondant icing

black cake-writing icing

yellow cake-writing icing

Preheat the oven to 180°C/350°F/Gas Mark 4. Put 12 paper baking cases in a bun tray, or put 12 double-layer paper cases on a baking tray.

Put the margarine, sugar, eggs and flour in a bowl and, using an electric hand whisk, beat together until smooth. Spoon the mixture into the cases.

Bake the cupcakes in the preheated oven for 15–20 minutes, or until well risen, golden brown and firm to the touch. Transfer to a wire rack and leave to cool.

When the cupcakes are cold, knead the orange icing until pliable, then roll out on a surface lightly dusted with icing sugar. Using the palm of your hand, lightly rub icing sugar into the icing to prevent it from spotting. Using a 5.5-cm/2¼-inch plain round cutter, cut out 12 circles, re-rolling the icing as necessary. Place a circle on top of each cupcake.

Roll out the black icing on a surface lightly dusted with icing sugar. Using the palm of your hand, lightly rub icing sugar into the icing to prevent it from spotting. Using a 3-cm/1¼-inch plain round cutter, cut out 12 circles and place them on the centre of the cupcakes. Using black writing icing, pipe 8 legs on to each spider and using white writing icing, draw 2 eyes and a mouth.

Valentine Heart Cupcakes

makes 6

85 g/3 oz butter, softened

85 g/3 oz caster sugar

½ tsp vanilla extract

2 eggs, lightly beaten

70 g/2½ oz plain flour

1 tbsp cocoa powder

1 tsp baking powder

for the marzipan hearts

35 g/1¼ oz marzipan

red food colouring
(liquid or paste)

icing sugar, for dusting

for the topping

55 g/2 oz butter, softened

115 g/4 oz icing sugar

25 g/1 oz plain chocolate,
melted

6 pink edible sugar flowers,
to decorate

To make the hearts, knead the marzipan until pliable, then add a few drops of red colouring and knead until evenly coloured. Roll out the marzipan to a thickness of 5 mm/¼ inch on a surface dusted with icing sugar. Using a small heart-shaped cutter, cut out 6 hearts. Place these on a tray, lined with greaseproof paper and dusted with icing sugar, and leave to dry for 3–4 hours.

To make the cupcakes, preheat the oven to 180°C/350°F/ Gas Mark 4. Put 6 paper muffin cases in a muffin tin.

Put the butter, sugar and vanilla extract in a bowl and beat together until light and fluffy. Gradually add the eggs, beating well after each addition. Sift in the flour, cocoa powder and baking powder and, using a large metal spoon, fold into the mixture. Spoon the mixture into the paper cases.

Bake the cupcakes in the preheated oven for 20–25 minutes, or until well risen and firm to the touch. Transfer to a wire rack and leave to cool.

To make the topping, put the butter in a large bowl and beat until fluffy. Sift in the icing sugar and beat together until smooth. Add the melted chocolate and beat together until well mixed. When the cupcakes are cold, spread the icing on top of each cupcake and decorate with a chocolate flower.

Cream Tea Cupcakes

makes 10

85 g/3 oz unsalted butter, softened

85 g/3oz caster sugar

½ tsp vanilla extract

1 large egg, lightly beaten

85 g/3 oz self-raising flour

1 tbsp milk

40 g/1½ oz raisins

115 g/4 oz small strawberries, hulled and sliced

1 tbsp strawberry conserve

115 g/4 oz clotted cream

icing sugar, for dusting

Preheat the oven to 190°C/375°F/Gas Mark 5. Put 10 paper baking cases in a bun tray or put 10 double-layer paper cases on a baking tray.

Put the butter, sugar and vanilla extract in a mixing bowl and beat together until light and fluffy. Gradually beat in the egg. Sift in the flour and, using a metal spoon, fold into the mixture with the milk and raisins. Spoon the mixture into the paper cases.

Bake the cupcakes in the preheated oven for 15–20 minutes or until golden brown and firm to the touch. Transfer to a wire rack and leave to cool.

When the cupcakes are cold, use a serrated knife to cut a circle from the top of each cupcake. Gently mix the strawberries and conserve together and divide between the cupcakes. Top each with a small dollop of clotted cream. Replace the cake tops and dust with icing sugar. Store the cupcakes in the refrigerator until ready to serve.

Feather-iced Coffee Cupcakes

makes 16

1 tbsp instant coffee granules

1 tbsp boiling water

115 g/4 oz butter, softened

115 g/4 oz soft light brown sugar

2 eggs

115 g/4 oz self-raising flour

½ tsp baking powder

2 tbsp soured cream

for the icing

225 g/8 oz icing sugar

4 tsp warm water

1 tsp instant coffee granules

2 tsp boiling water

Preheat the oven to 190°C/375°F/Gas Mark 5. Put 16 paper baking cases in 2 bun trays, or put 16 double-layer paper cases on a baking tray.

Put the coffee granules in a cup or small bowl, add the boiling water and stir until dissolved. Leave to cool slightly.

Put the butter, sugar and eggs in a bowl. Sift in the flour and baking powder, then beat the ingredients together until smooth. Add the dissolved coffee and the soured cream and beat together until well mixed. Spoon the mixture into the paper cases.

Bake the cupcakes in the preheated oven for 20 minutes, or until well risen and golden brown. Transfer to a wire rack and leave to cool.

To make the icing, sift 85 g/3 oz of the icing sugar into a bowl, then gradually mix in the warm water to make a coating consistency that will cover the back of a wooden spoon. Dissolve the coffee granules in the boiling water. Sift the remaining icing sugar into a bowl, then stir in the dissolved coffee granules. Spoon the icing into a piping bag fitted with a piping nozzle. When the cupcakes are cold, coat the tops with the white icing, then quickly pipe the coffee icing in parallel lines on top. Using a skewer, draw it across the piped lines in both directions. Leave to set before serving.

Marzipan Flower Cupcakes

makes 12

115 g/4 oz self-raising flour

½ tsp baking powder

115 g/4 oz soft tub margarine

115 g/4 oz caster sugar

2 eggs, lightly beaten

few drops almond extract

for the topping

200 g/7 oz marzipan

icing sugar, for dusting

2 tbsp apricot jam

Preheat the oven to 180°C/350°F/Gas Mark 4. Put 12 paper baking cases in a bun tray or put 12 double-layer paper cases on a baking tray.

Sift the flour and baking powder into a bowl. Add the margarine, sugar, eggs and almond extract and, using an electric hand whisk, beat together until smooth. Spoon the mixture into the paper cases.

Bake the cupcakes in the preheated oven for 20 minutes or until golden brown and firm to the touch. Transfer to a wire rack and leave to cool.

To top the cupcakes, roll out the marzipan on a surface dusted lightly with icing sugar. Using a 3-cm/1¼-inch round cutter, stamp out 60 circles, re-rolling the marzipan as necessary. Spread a little apricot jam over the top of each cupcake. Pinch the marzipan circles at one side to create petal shapes and arrange five petals on top of each cupcake. Roll small balls of remaining marzipan for the flower centres and place in the middle of the cupcakes.

Honey & Spice Cupcakes

makes 22–24

140 g/5 oz unsalted butter

100 g/3½ oz light muscovado sugar

100 g/3½ oz honey

200 g/7 oz self-raising flour

1 tsp ground allspice

2 eggs, beaten

22–24 whole blanched almonds

Preheat the oven to 180°C/350°F/Gas Mark 4. Place paper bun cases in two 12-cup shallow bun tins.

Place the butter, sugar and honey in a large saucepan and heat gently, stirring, until the butter is melted. Remove the pan from the heat.

Sift together the flour and allspice and stir into the mixture in the saucepan, then beat in the eggs, mixing to a smooth batter.

Spoon the batter into the prepared tins and place an almond on top of each one. Bake in the preheated oven for 20–25 minutes, or until well risen and golden brown. Transfer to a wire rack to cool.

Festive Cupcakes

makes 14

115 g/4 oz mixed dried fruit

1 tsp finely grated orange rind

2 tbsp brandy or orange juice

85 g/3 oz butter, softened

85 g/3 oz light soft brown sugar

1 large egg, lightly beaten

115 g/4 oz self-raising flour

1 tsp ground mixed spice

1 tbsp silver dragées (cake decoration balls), to decorate

for the icing

85 g/3 oz icing sugar

2 tbsp orange juice

Put the mixed fruit, orange rind and brandy or orange juice in a small bowl and cover and leave to soak for 1 hour.

Preheat the oven to 190°C/375°F/Gas Mark 5. Put 14 paper baking cases in 2 bun trays or put 14 double-layer paper cases on a baking tray.

Put the butter and sugar in a mixing bowl and beat together until light and fluffy. Gradually beat in the egg. Sift in the flour and mixed spice and, using a metal spoon, fold them into the mixture followed by the soaked fruit. Spoon the mixture into the paper cases.

Bake the cupcakes in the preheated oven for 15–20 minutes or until golden brown and firm to the touch. Transfer to a cooling rack and leave to cool.

To make the icing, sift the icing sugar into a bowl and gradually mix in enough orange juice until the mixture is smooth and thick enough to coat the back of a wooden spoon. Using a teaspoon, drizzle the icing in a ziz-zag pattern over the cupcakes. Decorate with the silver dragées. Leave to set.

Gold & Silver Anniversary Cupcakes

makes 24

225 g/8 oz butter, softened

225 g/8 oz caster sugar

1 tsp vanilla extract

4 large eggs, lightly beaten

225 g/8 oz self-raising flour

5 tbsp milk

for the topping

175 g/6 oz unsalted butter

350 g/12 oz icing sugar

25 g/1 oz silver or gold dragées (cake decoration balls)

Preheat the oven to 180°C/350°F/Gas Mark 4. Put 24 silver or gold foil cake cases in bun trays, or arrange them on baking trays.

Put the butter, sugar and vanilla extract in a bowl and beat together until light and fluffy. Gradually add the eggs, beating well after each addition. Add the flour and, using a large metal spoon, fold into the mixture with the milk. Spoon the mixture into the paper cases.

Bake the cupcakes in the preheated oven for 15–20 minutes, or until well risen and firm to the touch. Transfer to a wire rack and leave to cool.

To make the topping, put the butter in a large bowl and beat until fluffy. Sift in the icing sugar and beat together until well mixed. Put the topping in a piping bag, fitted with a medium star-shaped nozzle.

When the cupcakes are cold, pipe circles of icing on top of each cupcake to cover the tops. Sprinkle over the silver or gold dragées before serving.

Gold Star Cupcakes

makes 12

85 g/3 oz butter, softened

85 g/3 oz light soft brown sugar

1 large egg, beaten

85 g/3 oz self-raising flour

½ tsp ground cinnamon

1 tbsp milk

for the gold stars

85 g/3 oz yellow ready-to-roll coloured fondant

icing sugar, for dusting

edible gold dusting powder (optional)

for the icing

85 g/3 oz icing sugar

2–3 tsp lemon juice

Preheat the oven to 180°C/350°F/Gas Mark 4. Put 12 paper baking cases in a bun tray or put 12 double-layer paper cases on a baking tray.

Put the butter and sugar in a mixing bowl and beat together until light and fluffy. Gradually beat in the egg. Sift in the flour and cinnamon and, using a metal spoon, fold them into the mixture with the milk. Spoon the mixture into the paper cases.

Bake the cupcakes in the preheated oven for 20 minutes or until golden brown and firm to the touch. Transfer to a wire rack and leave to cool.

To make the gold stars, roll the yellow fondant out on a surface lightly dusted with icing sugar and, using a small star cutter, stamp out 12 stars. Brush each star with a little gold dusting powder, if using. Set aside on a sheet of baking parchment.

To make the icing, sift the icing sugar into a bowl and stir in enough lemon juice to make a smooth and thick icing.

Spoon the icing on top of the cupcakes and top each with a gold star. Leave to set.

Baby Shower Cupcakes with Sugared Almonds

makes 24

225 g/8 oz butter, softened

225 g/8 oz caster sugar

finely grated rind of 2 lemons

4 eggs, lightly beaten

225 g/8 oz self-raising flour

for the topping

350 g/12 oz icing sugar

red or blue food colouring (liquid or paste)

24 sugared almonds

Preheat the oven to 180°C/350°F/Gas Mark 4. Put 24 paper muffin cases in muffin tins.

Put the butter, sugar and lemon rind in a bowl and beat together until light and fluffy. Gradually add the eggs, beating well after each addition. Add the flour and, using a large metal spoon, fold into the mixture. Spoon the mixture into the paper cases to half-fill them.

Bake the cupcakes in the preheated oven for 20–25 minutes, or until well risen, golden brown and firm to the touch. Transfer to a wire rack and leave to cool.

When the cakes are cold, make the topping. Sift the icing sugar into a bowl. Add 6–8 teaspoons of hot water and stir until the mixture is smooth and thick enough to coat the back of a wooden spoon. Dip a skewer into the red or blue food colouring, then stir it into the icing until it is evenly coloured pink or pale blue.

Spoon the icing on top of each cupcake. Top each with a sugared almond and leave to set for about 30 minutes, before serving.

Easter Cupcakes

makes 12

115 g/4 oz butter, softened

115 g/4 oz caster sugar

2 eggs, lightly beaten

85 g/3 oz self-raising flour

25 g/1 oz cocoa powder

for the topping

85 g/3 oz butter, softened

175 g/6 oz icing sugar

1 tbsp milk

2–3 drops of vanilla extract

two 130 g/4¾ oz packets mini chocolate candy shell eggs

Preheat the oven to 180°C/350°F/Gas Mark 4. Put 12 paper baking cases in a bun tray, or put 12 double-layer paper cases on a baking tray.

Put the butter and sugar in a bowl and beat together until light and fluffy. Gradually add the eggs, beating well after each addition. Sift in the flour and cocoa powder and, using a large metal spoon, fold into the mixture. Spoon the mixture into the paper cases.

Bake the cupcakes in the preheated oven for 15–20 minutes, or until well risen and firm to the touch. Transfer to a wire rack and leave to cool.

To make the butter-cream topping, put the butter in a bowl and beat until fluffy. Sift in the icing sugar and beat together until well mixed, adding the milk and vanilla extract.

When the cupcakes are cold, put the icing in a piping bag, fitted with a large star nozzle, and pipe a circle around the edge of each cupcake to form a nest. Place chocolate eggs in the centre of each nest, to decorate.